Everything
You Need to
Know About

The Art of Leadership

How to Be a Positive Influence in Your Home, School, and Community

Leadership is a type of skill that helps you to work well with others.

Everything You Need to Know About

The Art of Leadership

How to Be a Positive Influence in Your Home, School, and Community

Holly Cefrey

The Rosen Publishing Group, Inc.
New York

To Richard, Elaine, and Ethan

Special thanks to Dean Galiano and the inspirational Rosen Group.

Published in 2000 by The Rosen Publishing Group, Inc.
29 East 21st Street, New York, NY 10010

Library of Congress Cataloging-in-Publication Data

Cefrey, Holly.
    Everything you need to know about the art of leadership: how to be a
    positive influence in your home, school, and community / by Holly Cefrey
      p. cm. — (The need to know library)
    Includes bibliographical references and index.
    Summary: Discusses the importance of having good leadership skills
    and outlines the abilities that help to become an effective leader.
    ISBN 0-8239-3217-6
    1. Leadership—Juvenile literature. [1. Leadership.] I. Title. II. Series
HM1261.C43 2000
303.3'4—dc21   99-048184
                                                   CIP
                                                   AC

Manufactured in the United States of America

Contents

Introduction

As we head toward the new millennium, it is interesting to look to the past and see how North American society has evolved. One of the things that has changed over the years is our growing acceptance of non-traditional role models as leaders. Traditionally, leaders were wealthy Caucasian males. Now as long as a person possesses the necessary skills required, almost anyone—regardless of gender, race, ethnicity, economic background, or disability—can be a leader.

The act of leading sets you apart from others. You are taking charge and guiding something or someone toward a goal. To be an effective leader, you need to develop the desire to get things done—to produce a positive outcome from your work. You must also be confident and have the ability to motivate others.

The ability to motivate others is essential to leadership.

However, this does not mean that leaders are better than followers. Most people, including leaders, guide people in some areas and follow people in other situations. Ultimately, the better you can follow, the better a leader you will become. You need to ask yourself, "Is this a positive, rewarding experience? If not, what could I do as a leader or follower to make it rewarding?" Sometimes the confidence that a leader has is enough to get others motivated, but a truly rewarding experience—as a leader or a follower—involves hard work.

Effective communication is another important factor in being a good leader. Ask yourself if you are able to communicate in a confident manner. What is your posture telling people about you? Are you able to tell others that their work is pleasing to you, and are you able to accept praise or criticism?

This book was written to help you develop your leadership qualities and skills, to use at school, at work, in your career, and in life.

Chapter One

Becoming a Leader

Since leaders are looked up to, it is important to project a good self-image by behaving with courtesy and confidence. Simple aspects of everyday behavior, like the way you dress, stand, and speak, send messages about who you are. People form impressions right away and decide, sometimes without knowing it, whether or not they want to listen to you.

Sending the Right Signals

Be aware of the silent signals you send. Suppose you have just started a job at a clothing store. If you go to work with your hair uncombed, wearing wrinkled clothes, and you seem bored, you will not project an image of being an enthusiastic worker. Your boss and

Customers are more responsive to employees who are articulate and enthusiastic.

those around you may very well doubt that you are interested in your job. Your boss may even ask you to reevaluate whether or not you want to continue working. On the other hand, if you dress appropriately, know about the merchandise, and act helpful but not too pushy, customers will seek your help. Eventually, the management will notice you. A professional presence and appearance will mark you as a leader.

As mentioned in the introduction, good communication is an important leadership tool. Speak as clearly as you can. Choose your words carefully, especially when saying something that you feel strongly about. When you are talking one-on-one, be polite, honest, and direct. Be sure to listen to what people say and let them know that you understand their concerns. If you are addressing a group, stand up straight and speak clearly.

Many people feel uncomfortable talking in front of a group of people. If you do, you may want to take a speech class or join an acting group to improve your public speaking. Even practicing in front of a mirror helps. Try to feel, or at least seem, at ease when you talk to a group.

Getting People's Attention

Alicia wanted to organize an Adopt-a-Grand-parent program for her high school and a neigh-

A speech class can help you to gain confidence speaking in front of others.

boring nursing home. She arranged a meeting for possible volunteers. After getting the volunteers' attention, Alicia realized that she was not sure what to say next. Embarrassed, she mumbled, "The adopt . . . program is . . . real important . . . " Eventually, she overcame her embarrassment and managed to say a few things about the program, but she could not help but notice that the volunteers kept looking at their watches and that they seemed bored. After the meeting, Alicia was discouraged because not many people signed up for the program.

Alicia decided to attend a meeting for the Baking for Baseball group that a friend of hers had organized. They were to hold weekly bake sales to earn money for baseball uniforms for the girls' team. Alicia watched as her friend Stephanie walked confidently to the podium, cleared her throat, and spoke in a strong, clear voice. Alicia marveled at how prepared Stephanie was.

Stephanie was able to get everyone's attention by showing that she had a clear purpose and the ability to lead the meeting. She was confident, well informed, and knew what she wanted to say before she addressed the group. Also, Stephanie was neatly dressed and well groomed. Now Alicia knew how she would prepare for the next meeting.

As a leader, you need to remember that time is very important to people, and when people are giving you some of their time, you need to make the most of it. Do your research before addressing a group. Practice out loud in your room. Make sure that you can follow through on what you say you will do. Sometimes people agree to lead projects and then abandon them. Try to be reliable; once you have agreed to something, do it!

Setting Goals

Part of leading is developing a plan and setting priorities. Suppose that you are working as a lifeguard at a pool and your supervisor asks you to be head lifeguard. One of your primary responsibilities is to teach the new lifeguards about the rules of the pool. You also need to figure out when to schedule their lunch breaks. Which topic are you going to address first? The safety rules, of course; they are a higher priority.

Remember to be reasonable when setting goals. For example, if you assigned tasks to the lifeguards that were not part of their job description, such as cleaning the bathrooms, they would probably resent you. As a good leader, it is important to find a healthy balance. If you ask people to do too much, they may burn out. If you ask them to do too little, they may feel undervalued.

Flexibility—the ability to adapt—is another characteristic of an effective leader. When someone approaches you with a difficulty, express your positive outlook by saying something like, "We can figure this out." If you are positive, others will trust you with their concerns and respect you for your ability to come up with reasonable solutions to problematic situations or conflicts.

If you respond to someone's problem by saying, "You did what? How stupid," people will not feel comfortable coming to you. As the leader, the responsibility of getting things worked out will ultimately fall on you. When all goes well, you will be credited for your good guidance.

Keep a positive attitude when people approach you with their problems.

Two Types of Power

Leaders can use two kinds of power to reach their goals. Formal power comes with a position. Examples of people with formal power include the boss in an office, the president of a club, or the teacher in a classroom. Informal power comes from popularity. If you are liked and respected, people are more likely to listen to you and want to work with you. Part of being a good leader is recognizing which type of power is available to you and learning how to use it.

Along with power, leading is a privilege. If people trust you to be their leader, you need to be worthy of their trust. This means that you must act morally, in ways that do not hurt others. You must make decisions that are ethical and considerate. Cheating or stealing has led to the downfall of people who were considered great leaders but are now remembered as traitors. Never forget that with privilege comes responsibility.

Chapter Two | Leaders Need Followers

As you develop and practice your leadership skills, remember that the nature of leadership is changing. The most successful companies and organizations no longer think that leaders should simply direct others. Leadership is about working with people, not over them. As a leader, you are expected to recognize good ideas from others and put them into action. You need to create an environment in which people know that their ideas are valuable.

At the art club meeting, Paula, the president, decided to let a volunteer lead the fund-raising group. Paula chose Crystal, who was excited to find out more about what she needed to do. "It's important that you try to remember everybody's name and ask for his or her fund-raising ideas," advised Paula.

At the next meeting, Crystal spoke to the other members. "My idea for raising funds is to make birthday cards and sell them at lunch. However, we are open to suggestions. There is a sign-up sheet on the door, and the first five students to sign the sheet will be on the fund-raising committee. We will meet here every Tuesday at three o'clock."

Crystal was on the right track for leadership. She knew to ask questions in order to make sure that she understood everything that Paula expected of her. When Crystal made the request for volunteers, she showed respect by saying, "I would like" rather than "I want." She also let the volunteers know what would be expected of them. That way, she would get informed volunteers who were ready to work.

Before the next meeting, Crystal read the sign-up sheet: "Susan, Trell, Riza, Phil, and Annie." She didn't know any of these students but was aware that once she met them, she needed to remember their names. As the students entered the meeting, Crystal played a memory game. She imagined things that would help her remember everybody. "I have a cousin named Susan, so when I meet Susan, I will think of my cousin," she thought. Trell was tall, so Crystal said "Tall Trell"

In social situations, make eye contact and try to remember people's names.

to herself as she was shaking Trell's hand. Riza was wearing a sweater that had eye-catching designs, so Crystal pretended that her sweater had pizza toppings on it. "Pizza Riza" she said to herself as Riza sat down. Crystal loved the musi-cal Annie, *so when she met Annie, she imagined her singing on a stage. When Crystal met Phil, she could not think of anything that would help her to remember, so she repeated Phil's name while looking at him: "Phil, it's nice to meet you. I can't wait to hear your ideas, Phil."*

By remembering their names, Crystal showed that she valued individual members. If you are not good at the memory game, try to write down whatever helps you to remember. If you try everything but forget a few names, do not feel bad. Saying, "I'm sorry. What is your name again?" and thanking the person once you are reminded is a polite way to recover.

The group had a lot of great ideas for raising funds. Even when their ideas were not so good, Crystal remained enthusiastic and thanked each member for his or her ideas. The entire group really liked her birthday card idea. Annie thought that it would be great to make all-occasion cards. Crystal agreed, "That's a great idea, Annie. Let's vote." Phil suggested that the members take turns selling the cards throughout the school year. "Wonderful idea, Phil. Although we will need permission from our principal, I think it could work," said Crystal.

Crystal gained the respect of the group by showing respect to the group. A great way to show respect is by listening. Good listening involves making eye contact and not interrupting the person who is speaking. Even if you totally disagree with what is said or do not like the person saying it, try to remain supportive and positive. At the very least, thank someone for his or her input. When you show that you appreciate what someone has said or done, everyone wins. When you thank people for their help, they feel rewarded and recognized. As a result, they are more likely to help in the future. Thoughtful behavior adds to your image as a leader because you seem sensitive, gracious, and confident.

Prioritize your tasks and see if any of your responsibilities can be given to others.

Delegating Tasks

If you are leading a large project or working with a lot of people, be sure to delegate responsibilities clearly. When you ask a specific person to do a task, let her or him know exactly what is involved. Check back later to see if there are any problems. If you try to do everything yourself, you exclude others and exhaust yourself. As an effective leader, you need to keep people involved. Try to find ways to make the most of people's talents; people power is too valuable to waste.

A leader must try to inspire others to work together. Never position people against one another. Let's say that you are running for class treasurer, and you hold a meeting for campaign volunteers. It would not be smart to divide your volunteers into two groups, asking each to come up with a slogan so that you can choose one. The group whose slogan you didn't choose might feel hurt or resentful. How you achieve a goal is as important as succeeding. Have everyone work on creating a slogan together: This process is called creative brainstorming. Try to make the session fun. Bring markers so people can draw images to go with their words. If the group is small and you can afford it, bring along some snacks. Make sure that you know everyone, and then introduce people to each other.

People lead best by example. Your actions show the importance that you place on a certain task. Pour your

Enlist the help of friends when campaigning for student government.

energy into reaching your goal, and your commitment will inspire the actions of others.

Experts have divided leadership skills into three broad categories:

- diagnostic skills: critical and creative thinking and problem solving

- perceptual skills: communicating well through good verbal and listening skills

- behavioral skills: teamwork, negotiation, delegation, motivation, coaching, and counseling

As you can see, leadership involves many different skills. Some of these may come naturally to you; you may need to work on others. You will be an effective leader if you can use your strengths and work on your weaknesses.

If you are not sure what your strengths and weaknesses are, think about the last time you solved a problem. The steps that you took to solve the problem are your strengths. Your weaknesses are the things that you did not do to prevent the problem or ways in which you were unable to identify and solve the problem earlier. However, the ability to work on your weaknesses is a strength in itself.

Chapter Three

School: An Opportunity to Lead

School is a great place to learn leadership skills. As you study and have fun with your friends, you also have the chance to explore your interests. Taking classes and trying activities will help you figure out what you may want to do later in life. Following your interests can lead you to opportunities in which you can learn to be a capable leader.

School: A Leader's Laboratory

At school you have a community of people gathered to accomplish goals: learning, teaching, or working. You can find a number of leaders in school. By watching and becoming involved, you can find out what makes a strong leader.

Teachers who keep students engaged are effective leaders.

The way to begin is by observing. Look at the adults in positions of authority: the principal, the teachers, and the counselors. Who is the most respected? As you go through your classes, take the time to note effective leadership styles. Why does one teacher keep a class's attention, whereas another has the same students daydreaming?

You will probably discover some similarities among the teachers who are great leaders. First, they are committed to their subject matter. Second, they respect the students. This means not only talking to them with courtesy but also listening to them with consideration. Third, they are prepared. They don't just come into class and ramble on. They have a thought-out lesson plan.

You may notice other individual factors that contribute to impressive leadership. A teacher may use humor to interest students. Another teacher might have a way of talking that makes the material more interesting. Perhaps the most powerful way for any leader to get someone's attention is to address the listener's concerns.

Listening and Learning

Every time Tim mentioned the winter carnival in class assembly, he lost control of the students. The class was split on where to hold the carnival: Some students thought that it should be in front of the school, and others wanted to have it in the back parking lot. Some students didn't want a carnival at all. Instead, they wanted to go skiing. Finally Tim decided to make the decision on his own. After all, he was the elected president.

"We will have a winter carnival, and it will be held in the front parking lot," he announced.

Many students left the assembly after Tim said this. He couldn't figure out what he had done wrong. The remaining students were still arguing.

"They couldn't make a decision, so I made it for them," Tim reasoned.

"You made a decision before listening to the reasons why the students had three different opinions," said Elaine, vice president of the class.

Tim printed up a pamphlet urging the students to attend the next school assembly. He wrote that they still needed to make a decision regarding the carnival, despite what he had said in the last meeting. He created a schedule in which the three groups, with their differing opinions, would get fifteen minutes each to present their proposals. Then everyone would vote to see which suggestion was the most popular.

At the next school assembly, Tim asked the students to remain quiet during the group presentations. After the presentations were finished, Tim said, "Each group has great ideas. We will vote for one of the three choices." The majority of students

School can provide opportunities to lead activities and projects.

voted for the ski trip. After the assembly, many of the students thanked Tim for listening.

Using Ambition

If you are reading this book, you have ambition. How do you use your ambition in school? Do you study hard so that you can get into a good college? Do you exercise in order to do well on a sports team? These are positive uses of ambition. Sometimes, however, ambition can take over your sense of reason, making you harm yourself or others.

Kara's older sister, Bette, was a well-known track star. This was Kara's first year on the junior track team. Because of Bette's good reputation,

Kara was elected team captain. Kara thought that she remembered everything Bette had told her about track, but she was in for a big surprise.

One day, Heidi approached Kara. Heidi had been on the junior team when Bette was on varsity. "We're excited that you're on the team. If you're anything like your sister, you'll take us to the finals. Bette used these for an extra edge," said Heidi as she showed Kara a handful of pills.

"Are those vitamins?" asked Kara.

Heidi laughed. "No, these are bennies. They make you go real fast," she said. "How do you think your sister got that scholarship?" she asked as the other girls nodded their heads. "Here, take some before you run," she said, handing Kara the pills. Kara put the pills in her sock and returned to the junior team warm-up. Her teammates were impressed that Kara had been talking to the varsity team.

If her sister had used the pills, Kara thought, maybe she should, too. Kara took a friend aside and said, "They gave me pills that they said my sister used."

"Really?" asked her friend. "I don't think that sounds like your sister. You need to be careful. Drugs can do serious harm to your body. They can even affect your mind and speech. I don't think you should take them, Kara."

Joining a club or team is a first step toward achieving a leadership position.

There is a strong possibility that Kara could be expelled if she takes the drugs. However, powerful ambition can lead people to make foolish decisions. That is what happened to Bette. Sometimes people want to succeed so badly that they will do anything for it, even if it means hurting themselves or doing something illegal. You need to keep your ambition focused on positive goals and avoid destructive behavior.

Using Opportunities

Perhaps the most important factor in leadership is simply taking advantage of the chance to lead. The clubs, teams, and classes that take place at school need leadership if anything positive is to happen.

New leaders are always in demand because the student population is always changing. Do not be afraid to try for leadership positions. It is better to try and fail than to do nothing at all.

Sharon was quiet and shy, but when it came to computers, she would jump at the chance to help other students with their computer questions. She wished that instead of going home after school, she could stay in the computer lab. When she was working with computers, she was happy and confident about who she was. Ms. Leary, the lab teacher, talked with Sharon a lot about computers. It was the only time in school when Sharon spoke more than a few sentences at a time.

One day, Sharon asked Ms. Leary if the lab could start a computer club. "What a good idea. You would make a great club president," Ms. Leary said. Sharon paused. She hadn't envisioned herself as president.

"President? That's so hard," whined Sharon.

"I have an idea, Sharon," said Ms. Leary, "I realize that being president seems like too much right now. How about we put you in charge of getting people to join the club? Maybe you could run for secretary or treasurer; then you won't have as much responsibility as the president. Either way, the club will benefit from your enthusiasm."

Think about the special strengths
you can bring to a leadership role.

When Sharon told the lab students about the
club, they were excited. "I nominate Sharon for
president," Todd said.

Sharon felt her heart beat faster. "No . . . no, I
can't run for president. I am in charge of getting
students to join." It was an excuse that Sharon
was glad to use.

Some of the students seemed disappointed.
Sharon couldn't figure out why they would ever
want her as president. There were so many popular students that could easily win.

Sharon didn't know that a popular person does
not always make the best leader. People like to get
involved with leaders who have a passion for their

cause. Sharon's computer savvy made her an authority—even though she was shy.

Throughout the year, Sharon wrote speeches for the president and organized club events. After learning exactly what a club officer did, the next year she ran for president. She realized that the previous year, she had let her fear of losing and lack of confidence prevent her from representing something that she loved: computers. She was excited and surprised when she won the election.

Learning About Yourself

You may surprise yourself, too, as you take on leadership roles in school. Future college and job applications will ask about your involvement in extracurricular activities. If you have been a leader, you will be perceived as someone with vision, commitment, and the drive to succeed. You will be prepared to take a leadership position in your future career.

Chapter Four

Setting the Pace in the Workplace

In the Broadway musical *How to Succeed in Business Without Really Trying,* a window washer named J. Pierrepont Finch rises to the head of a large company without doing much work. Instead, he looks as though he is busy but really spends his time getting noticed and liked by the company president. Finch is constantly saying and spelling his name so that the people in power will remember him. As the final curtain comes down, Finch is the president of the board of trustees.

All of this creates a great musical comedy, but in real life, making your way to the top is not so easy. If you want to move up the ladder at work, you need to be able to do your job. Doing a job well is the first step toward leadership in a future career.

Arriving to work on time shows that you are responsible.

Practicing Leadership

In junior high and high school, you probably will not get a job that puts you right into a leadership position. At this point in your life, you do not yet have the necessary experience or time to lead a company. In any work situation, however, you can still set yourself apart as a leader.

To do this, you need to have positive work habits. Always arrive at work on time. A prompt arrival sends a meaningful signal to your employer. It lets your boss know that you are reliable and ready to work. The boss can count on you to be there and get the job done.

Present yourself well through the way you look and act. The way you dress creates a significant impression.

Although the clothing required to work in a fast-food restaurant varies from what is appropriate in a business office, some common guidelines apply. Look at what the other employees are wearing, and dress similarly. You may need to buy some key wardrobe items, such as dark pants or a white shirt, but a few well-chosen pieces combined in different ways can work. Minor details, like wearing a belt or socks, do a lot to show that you care about the business's image. Consider the professional world before getting tattoos or body piercings. If you already have tattoos or body piercings, cover them up or leave the piercing rings at home.

Good communication is important. Speak to everyone—customers, supervisors, and coworkers—with courtesy. The simple use of manners, such as saying please and thank you, may be what makes you stand out. When you are asked a question that requires a detailed answer, respond with more than yes or no. Listen carefully when you are given a task to complete; take notes if necessary. Ask questions if you need to, but once you understand what you are being asked to do, go to work.

Perhaps the most critical factor that can mark you as a leader is your attitude. Do you seem eager to do your job well? Try to avoid careless mistakes. Review your work before showing it to others. If you have extra time and you want more responsibility, speak up. Look for ways to stay productive and involved.

Handling Conflict

Conflict can be caused by limitations that prevent a final goal from being achieved, such as budget problems, an uncooperative worker, or a scheduling problem. Moral issues—like on-the-job theft—can cause conflicts, too. There are also people who crave constant conflict, and sometimes they bring this craving into the group environment. A good leader figures out ways to handle different types of conflict.

Sarah had been watching a group of workers in the corner of the office. It seemed as if they spent most of their time gossiping or making loud noises that distracted other coworkers. Sarah was the newly appointed team leader, which meant that she needed to do something about this behavior to make the environment productive for all of the employees. Some workers in the group were older than she was; she had a hard time picturing herself scolding someone who was ten years older. The company had not really trained her to handle this kind of problem. When she asked her boss what to do, Joe said, "Let's see what solution you come up with on your own."

Sarah agonized over what to do. She asked her family, which did not help much. One day she was listening to her boss praise a usually late coworker for arriving on time. This gave Sarah

Make yourself visible to managers and coworkers.

an idea. She watched the group carry on and focused on the loudest member, Matt. Sarah put together a folder with Matt's work history and accomplishments.

Sarah told Matt that she would like to speak with him. At their meeting, Sarah said, "Please have a seat. The company has always been happy with your work. I see from your resume that you enjoy hiking on weekends. That must be fun." Sarah smiled.

Matt, not sure what the meeting was for, smiled back and said, "Hiking is my exercise."

"I have asked you here," Sarah continued, "because we need someone to set a good example for the team. Since your work is great, we would like you to do it."

Matt tilted his head and listened carefully.

"We need a well-balanced employee, someone whose projects show concern for the work, and whose office behavior does not distract others, and I think that you are the best person to set the example. What do you think?" she asked.

No one from work had ever made Matt feel important before. "Yes, that would be great," he said.

Matt returned to the corner, where his coworkers were waiting to hear about the meeting. "Oh, we were just counting how many vacation days I have coming," Matt joked. "Hmm. I have to get to work on this file," he said as he quietly turned toward his desk.

Sarah discussed her solution with Joe. Joe congratulated Sarah on her ability to solve the problem. Joe said that if Matt kept up his good behavior, the company would assign him more important projects in the future.

Being Visible

If you do your job well, the people who work with you will notice your commitment. This includes your manager or supervisor. A sensible manager will do what is necessary to keep you around, whether that means a raise, a promotion, or simply steady employment. If your supervisor is not often in the workplace, do not just put on a show of hard work when he or she shows up.

Ethan had been mowing his family's lawn since he was twelve years old. He knew about the importance of safety when using dangerous equipment. Now that he was sixteen, he wanted to get a summer job mowing lawns. In order to do so, he needed a parent's permission. The mowing company that accepted his application wanted to put him through a week-long safety course.

"I already know what we are going to cover in

the course," he told his mom. "I think I'll try another company."

"Even though you think you know all about safety," said Ethan's mom, "this course is a good opportunity for your employers to see how dedicated and enthusiastic you are."

Ethan took the course as his mom had suggested, and he realized that it was a great way for the company to get to know him.

After receiving wonderful comments about Ethan from the course instructor, the boss assigned Ethan to a team that mowed lawns in the most expensive neighborhoods. Ethan worked with three other employees. Two of them were in college, and the other was the boss's niece. Ethan was surprised when the niece and one of the college students would take long breaks, sometimes leaving to go for a swim nearby. Jamie, the remaining employee, explained why this happened.

"They have been working for the company for five years. They're slackers, but the boss doesn't come by to check on us. We could slack, too, but I work hard because once I have worked for this company for a while, I plan to leave and start my own."

Ethan had two choices. He could remain a hard worker or slack off like his coworkers.

At the end of the summer, Ethan was glad

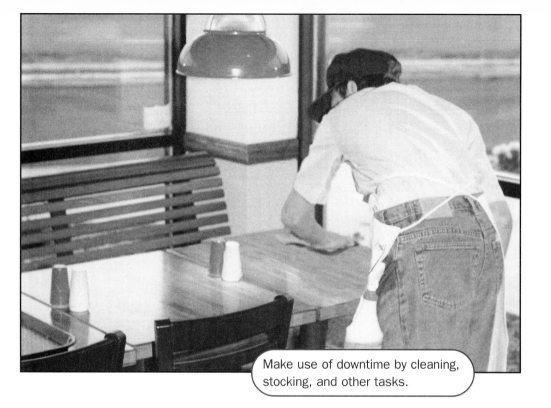

Make use of downtime by cleaning, stocking, and other tasks.

that he had made the right choice. One day the boss drove by, and of course his niece and her coworker were nowhere to be found. Jamie and Ethan said that they didn't know where they had gone. When the niece and coworker returned, Ethan thought for sure the boss would let them have it.

"Well, kids, that's no way to work," said the boss.

Ethan waited until he could speak to the boss alone. "Why aren't you mad that they have been goofing off?" asked Ethan.

His boss replied, "I can't be too hard on them. You are a great worker, but it is hard to find kids your age with your kind of dedication. It's also hard to find college kids who are still willing to mow lawns on their summers off. So I have to reward those who work hard for me and hope that the others catch on."

Ethan received a big bonus for all of his hard work, as did Jamie. Over the next couple of years, the boss taught them how to run a business and decided to help them start their own house-painting company.

Show Initiative

No matter where you are working, you can take the initiative and start doing something that will improve the work you do. For example, if you are a baby-sitter, you might pick up the children's toys after they are asleep. If you deliver newspapers, be sure that they make it to the doorstep. Customers and employers appreciate good quality and service.

Every job offers you a learning opportunity. A bad work experience can teach you how not to run a business or what to do differently as a boss. If you are lucky, you may find work that helps you move toward your career. However, you can make the most of any work situation by developing your leadership skills.

Chapter Five

Moving Forward in Your Career

Have you thought about what you might choose as your life's work? Some students know from an early age what they would like to become; others take many years to decide. Either way, you can use your qualities and skills as a leader to help you explore different careers.

Getting Educated

A good education is a great asset. There are true stories of successful people who did not go to school beyond the eighth grade, but they are rare. Usually people who do not graduate from high school find their career choices very limited.

A strong educational background looks impressive

on a job application or resume. It shows that you can concentrate and fulfill your goal by graduating. The more education you get, whether through high school, technical school, community courses, or college, the better off you will be. In addition to your studies, you can get a valuable education outside the classroom. Organizations in your neighborhood, such as your church, synagogue, or volunteer fire department, offer chances to become a leader.

By volunteering at an agency or organization, you can learn about the work involved. Perhaps you can get an internship at a company. By talking with people who have careers that appeal to you, you can learn the satisfying and frustrating aspects of those occupations.

Sabella's brother Jake always talked about how easy their aunt's job was. Their aunt, Talia, owned an apartment building and taught a real estate class. "All you have to do is buy a building, and then you're on easy street for life," Jake said. Sabella had a feeling that there was more to it than that, since their aunt was always busy.

Talia was known in their community because she taught classes on real estate. Sabella wanted to see for herself what it would be like to own an apartment building. She asked Talia if she and Jake could attend the classes.

"You can come, but the meetings are more for

adults," Talia said. "You have a vacation coming up. Why don't you both spend time with me then and see what I do?"

Jake went to one of the meetings. After attending the meeting, he was discouraged. "You have to get permission from the city to do things, and it took two hours just to cover that stuff," he said.

Sabella was still curious. "If it's so hard, why would someone want to do it?" Sabella asked her aunt why she owned an apartment building.

"I get a wonderful sense of pride knowing that I can provide places for people to live," Talia answered. "The government gave me special consideration for being a minority and a woman. I have had all sorts of help learning how to be a leader in the community. It's a lot of work, and there is always something new to learn, but I like a challenge. I set a good example for others, and I try to be good to my tenants and employees," she continued. "The classes allow me to give something of what I have learned and benefited from back to the community. In fact, I attended a community class, which started this whole thing for me," she said.

Sabella observed her aunt during her week's vacation. Sabella was surprised at how much was involved in owning an apartment building. She

Asking for assistance from others can help you to achieve your own goals.

saw how her aunt delegated responsibilities to her employees. Sabella decided that she would like to own an apartment building someday.

"No matter what you do, your work will always benefit from proper organization," her aunt said. "You need to take the time to do the little things as well as the big things. If I had poor organizational skills, I would have quit being a community leader a long time ago."

Having a Mentor

Sabella could ask Talia to be her mentor. A mentor is someone who helps you advance from one point in your life to another. Mentors have experience and can teach you about a field or profession. Students can join mentoring programs set up by their schools or the companies where they work. You can make the most of a program by meeting with your mentor regularly. Ask your mentor how he or she obtained his or her present position. What would the mentor recommend that you do or be careful not to do? Learn the key to your mentor's success, and see if it can open doors for you.

If you are not part of a formal mentoring program, you can still find someone to be your mentor. This might include a teacher, a cleric, or a relative. Is there someone whom you respect for his or her accomplishments? If so, ask that person for guidance. You can meet mentors through volunteering. You can also ask parents, teachers, or counselors to help you find a role model. Even the process of finding a mentor can help you develop leadership skills.

Coaching Others

You might act as a mentor yourself by coaching someone else. Although coaching is usually associated with sports teams, it actually involves helping and encouraging others to reach any goal. If there is someone you know who needs help studying a subject or practicing for a competition in an area in which you have ability or experience, you can coach this person and practice leading one-on-one. You might also help coach a local soccer or Little League team and closely observe the leadership styles of other coaches. Tell a teacher or counselor about your interest in gaining leadership skills. He or she will be able to advise you on programs like Big Brothers/Big Sisters or school tutoring programs. If your school does not have a tutoring program, perhaps you can start one.

Remember that praising people for what they do right usually encourages them to try to do it well again. Coaches, tutors, and advisers who put others down end up discouraging them. Insulting players or participants results in less team spirit and less drive to succeed. Praising what is being done right, and then instructing what can be done better, inspires the people you are coaching to move ahead.

Talk to family members and other adults for advice on career planning.

Making Connections

As you move ahead in your work, get to know people in your field. When you are looking for a job or seeking a better position, you increase your chances of getting it if you know someone who makes the hiring or promoting decisions. If you do not yet know anyone who does what you would like to do, find a way to meet people in that field.

Try to get involved with a company that interests you. Once you are there, show your potential as a leader. Do your work well. When you appreciate a supervisor, let him or her know. You could send a note about what you have learned. If you move to another department or company, stay in touch. Keeping these connections can be useful later in your career.

Chapter Six

Mastering the Art of Leadership

*R*ichard has worked for Lucent Technologies *for thirty-seven years. He is a department chief. He oversees section chiefs who are responsible for organizing the hundreds of employees who work in each department. Although Richard has always had a desire to lead, he developed successful leadership skills through years of practice and hard work. His views on leadership reflect the writings of this book.*

It is easy for a leader to use the excuse that there are too many people to know individually, so why bother? Richard stresses the importance of not following that kind of thinking.

"A good leader finds ways to remember the people who work with and for that leader," he

A good leader works hard and treats employees with respect.

says. "I find ways to meet each person. I involve myself in paycheck pickup. Employees come to me to get their paychecks. I meet each person and make him or her feel that I am very approachable," Richard says. "Our company celebrates anniversaries of when people were hired. I make sure that I respect each employee's anniversary and hand out gifts of appreciation." This kind of environment establishes happy individuals working as a whole, which makes for easier leading."

Leaders of large companies may become unapproachable because of their workload. And sometimes, the power of leading can go to their head. Being unapproachable can be a problem because when you lead like this, you become a figurehead.

Richard adds, "This happens when people feel that they can't talk to you, so they talk about you. When you become a leader, you act as a goodwill ambassador. A good leader should be able to be nurturing and compassionate. Make sure that you involve yourself with all concerns of your employees—whether small or large. You gain respect from employees by doing something about their issues."

Many factors can vary the success of a workplace leader. Both company policies and workloads can change, but the most important factor is the effort that people put into their work. As a leader, what do you do if you have careless followers? Richard's view on dealing with less-than-satisfactory people is something that we can apply to daily life: "Even if someone is not helpful or generally not nice to work with, do everything you can to show that you are nice to work with. If an employee is unpleasant or careless, it is a good indication that they are experiencing difficulties at work or in their private life. This is a perfect opportunity for a leader to use their skills. You make every effort to address the issues that are causing the employee to behave improperly. Then you can rest knowing that you are no longer responsible for this person's problems. If you treat others how you would like to be treated, you can't go wrong."

Glossary

accomplish To achieve a goal.

ambition Drive to succeed.

appoint To assign officially.

approachable Being easy to meet or talk with.

authority An expert, or to have power and influence.

burn out To stop working because of overwork.

capability Skill, know-how, potential.

commitment Dedication, follow-through.

communicate To share thoughts, feelings, and information with others.

delegate To assign tasks and responsibilities.

figurehead Someone who has a title with no responsibility or who is not approachable.

formal power Power that comes from holding a position, as with a boss or teacher.

goodwill ambassador A representative with a friendly desire for things to go well.

informal power Power that comes from popularity.

initiative The drive to start up or begin something.

leader Someone able to influence others and get things done.

mentor An instructor.

motivate To get people excited about something, inspiring them to take action.

negotiate To work with others to settle a matter.

priority A main concern.

privilege An honor.

proposal A planned offer.

reliable Believable, dependable.

Where to
Go for Help

In the United States

Boys and Girls Club
National Headquarters
1230 West Peachtree Street NW
Atlanta, GA 30309
(404) 815-5700
Web site: http://www.bgca.org

Do Something
423 West 55th Street, 8th Floor
New York, NY 10019
(212) 523-1175
Web site: http://www.dosomething.org
The Do Something Web site teaches you how to get involved in leadership activities relating to spirit, education, health, economy, and government under its community builder section.

The National Mentoring Partnership
1400 I Street NW, Suite 850
Washington, DC 20005
(202) 729-4345
Web site: http://www.mentoring.org
The National Mentoring Partnership Web site answers questions about mentoring and will help you find a mentor.

YMCA of the USA
101 North Wacker Drive
Chicago, IL 60606
(800) 872-9622
Web site: http://www.ymca.net

In Canada

Anger Management Counseling Practice of Toronto
603 Clinton Street
Toronto, Ontario M6G 2Z2
(416) 537-8654
Web site: http://www.anger.on.ca

YMCA Canada
42 Charles Street East, 6th Floor
Toronto, Ontario M4Y 1T4
(416) 967-9622
Web site: http://www.ymca.ca/home.htm

Web Sites

The Boys and Girls Clubs of America
http://www.ncnatural.com/ucyouth/index.html

Congressional Youth Leadership Council
http://www.cylc.org

Future Business Leaders of America
http://www.fbla-pbl.org

Girl Power
http://www.girlpower.com

The National Association for Community Leadership
http://www.communityleadership.org

Youth Link
http://www.youthlink.org

For Further Reading

Allen, Zita. *Black Women Leaders of the Civil Rights Movement.* Danbury, CT: Franklin Watts, 1996.

Erlbach, Arlene. *The Kids' Business Book.* Minneapolis, MN: Lerner Publications Co., 1998.

Frisch, Carlienne. *Everything You Need to Know About Getting a Job.* New York: Rosen Publishing Group, 2000.

Lewis, Barbara, Pamela Espeland, and Caryn Pernu. *The Kids' Guide to Social Action: How to Solve the Social Problem You Choose.* Minneapolis: MN: Free Spirit Press, 1998.

Mayo, Patty, and Pattii Waldo. *Scripting: Social Communication for Adolescents.* 2nd ed. Eau Claire, WI: Thinking Publications, 1994.

Phifer, Paul. *Great Careers in Two Years.* Chicago, IL: Ferguson Publishing Company, 2000.

Reeves, Diane Lindsey. *Career Ideas for Kids.* New York: Facts on File, 1999.

Sommers, Annie Leah. *Effective Communication at School and at Work.* New York: Rosen Publishing Group, 2000.

Index

About the Author

Holly Cefrey attended the University of Nebraska before moving to New York. She is a freelance writer, researcher, and artist. She also auditions for television commercials.

Photo Credits

Cover by Kristen Artz. P. 10 © Skjold International. All other photos by Matthew Baumann and Kim Sonsky.

Design and Layout

Annie O'Donnell